LEARN AS YOU PLAY FLUTE

BY PETER WASTALL

Revised edition 1989

Learn As You Play is a series of instrumental tutors designed
specifically to prepare pupils for the early grades of all
the principal examination boards. The tutors are suitable for
both individual and group instruction.

The course, which is divided into 24 units,
places the maximum emphasis on the early development
of musicianship. From the beginning it introduces the
student to a wide range of music, including works
by leading contemporary composers. Each unit contains
the following teaching programme:

1

New material is presented in clear progressive steps

2

Short, concise exercises enable new skills
to be quickly developed

3

Instrumental solos by distinguished composers
stimulate and develop practice repertoire

4

Progressive technical studies gradually bring the student
into contact with specific instrumental technique

5

Instrumental duets (alternate units) provide experience
in ensemble playing. Keyboard accompaniments
to the duets can be added in early units

Progress is measured at eight-unit intervals
by the introduction of Concert Pieces which utilise
all previously learned material

Piano accompaniments are available for these pieces
in a separate accompaniment book. The Concert Pieces
are works representative of examination requirements
and in many instances are works which have been set
in current or past syllabuses.

SERIES EDITOR
PETER WASTALL

BOOSEY & HAWKES

Head joint

To assemble the head joint align with the body tube so that the embouchure hole is in a direct line with the left hand first finger tone hole. Where alignment marks are incorporated into the flute design use the centre marks unless recommended otherwise by a teacher.

Body tube

Embouchure hole

Lip plate

First

B♭ key

Thum

Hand positions

Notice the left hand first finger supporting the flute

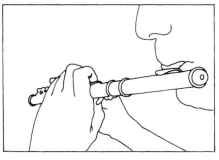

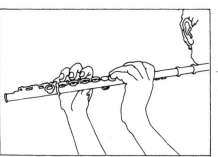

Notice the curve of the left hand positioning the fingers over the flute

Thumb positions

Notice how the right thumb supports the flute

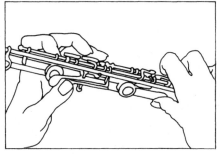

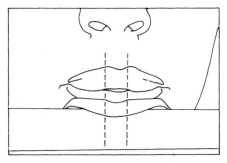

Notice how the left thumb supports the flute

Lip positions

As a general rule, the lower lip should cover about one third of the embouchure hole.

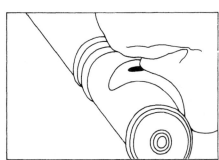

As a general rule, the width of the aperture should be approximately equal to the width of the embouchure hole

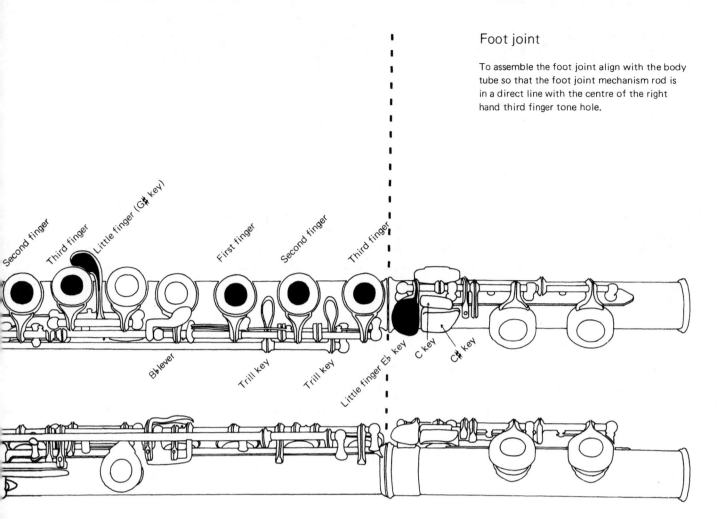

Foot joint

To assemble the foot joint align with the body tube so that the foot joint mechanism rod is in a direct line with the centre of the right hand third finger tone hole.

Using the picture as a guide for your fingers, compare the sounds of G, A, B and C.

Start each note with a tongue movement similar to that used when pronouncing the letter 'T'

			G	A	B	C
Closed ●						
Open ○						
Left hand	Thumb	First finger	● ●	● ●	● ●	○ ●
		Second finger	● ●	● ●	● ○	○
		Third finger	●	○	○	○
Right hand		First finger	○	○	○	○
		Second finger	○	○	○	○
		Third finger	○	○	○	○
		Little finger	E♭ key	E♭ key	E♭ key	E♭ key

PREPARATORY MATERIAL FOR UNIT 1

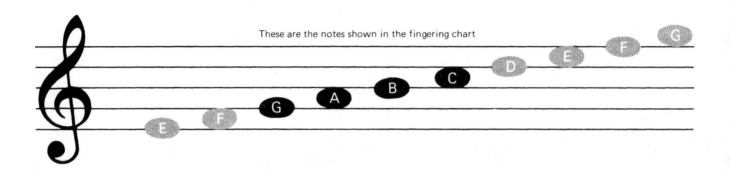

These are the notes shown in the fingering chart

Notation

Printed notes are also named after the first seven letters of the alphabet. From the example it can be seen that they are placed on a staff (the name of the five lines), each line and each space counting as one letter name.

The Treble Clef

Since the same seven letter names are used for all instruments (i.e. those that produce low notes, as well as those that produce high notes) a clef sign is placed at the beginning of each staff to establish exact pitch. Music for the flute uses the treble clef.

Note Lengths

The length of time a note is played is measured by the beat; the difference in length being shown by various types of note. The three types used in unit 1 are:

crotchet   minim   semibreve

Play the following crotchets trying to hold each for exactly the same amount of time.

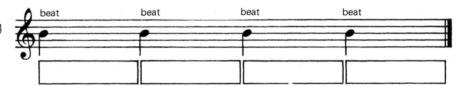

Now play the following minims, holding each note for the whole of beats one and two added together.

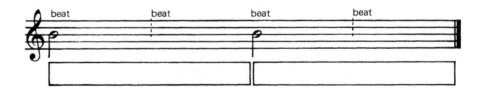

Now play a semibreve, trying to hold the note for exactly four beats.

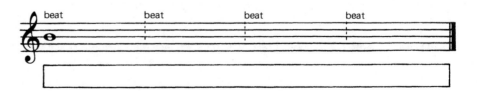

4

Bars and bar lines

Bar line   Double bar line

Beats usually group themselves into regular patterns of either two, three or four; to show these patterns, the music is divided by bar lines into bars.

A double bar-line is used to separate differing sections of music within a single piece.

A thin/thick double bar indicates the end of a piece or exercise.

Time Signatures

A time-signature is placed at the beginning of each piece of music to show how many beats there are in a bar, and the type of note that equals one beat. It is printed in fractional form, the value of the crotchet being shown as a fraction of a semibreve.

2/4 showing 2 crotchet beats in each bar

3/4 showing 3 crotchet beats in each bar

4/4 showing 4 crotchet beats in each bar

UNIT 1

Notes and Fingerings
(summarised from p. 2 – 5)

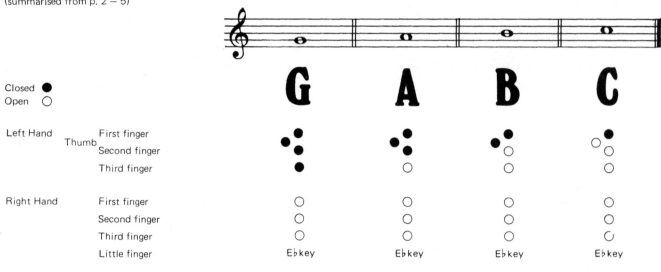

Closed ●
Open ○

Left Hand — Thumb — First finger
Second finger
Third finger

Right Hand — First finger
Second finger
Third finger
Little finger

Exercise 1

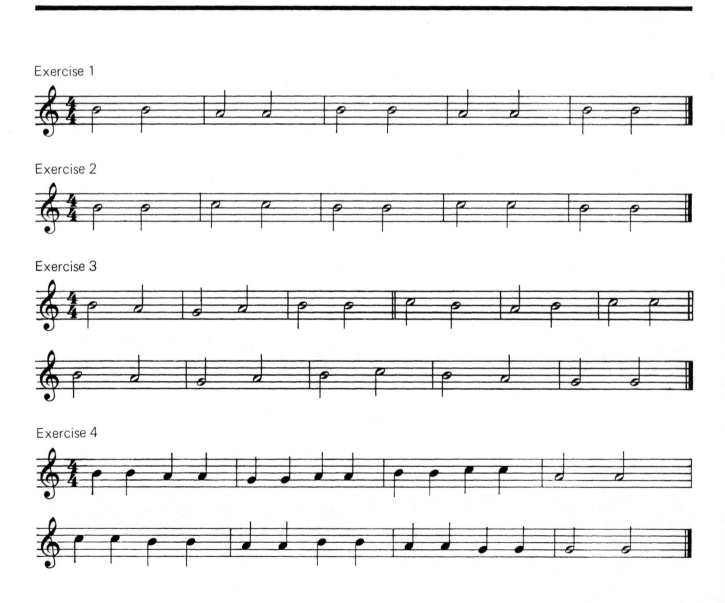

Exercise 2

Exercise 3

Exercise 4

Exercise 5

Musicianship

When you practise the instrumental solos, notice how the notes form patterns almost as if they were words in a rhyme. In music these note patterns are called phrases; to help to identify them, phrases in some early pieces have been marked with brackets. Breaths are normally taken at the ends of phrases; additional breaths can be taken, but these must be discreet so as not to disturb the natural flow of the phrase.

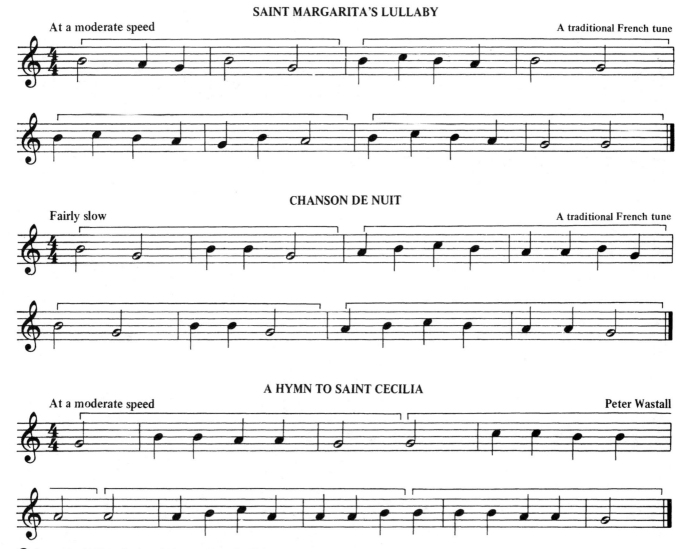

SAINT MARGARITA'S LULLABY

At a moderate speed   A traditional French tune

CHANSON DE NUIT

Fairly slow   A traditional French tune

A HYMN TO SAINT CECILIA

At a moderate speed   Peter Wastall

UNIT 2

The Pause sign

Rests

When a pause sign is placed over a note, the beat stops and the note is played for a period of time longer than its printed value. During the first section of this book the pause will be used mainly in the tone development exercises, identifying individual notes that are to be sustained for as long as possible.

The length of time in which notes are not played is shown by various rests, each note having an equivalent rest. The example shows the minim rest (two beats of silence) and the crotchet rest (one beat of silence).

Exercise 1

Exercise 2

Exercise 3

MINUETTO

Fairly fast

Adapted from a minuet
by James Hook

Tone development

One of the best ways to develop a full tone is to play individual long notes. In the exercise that follows, carry out the following drill.

1. Listen closely to the sound, aiming for a full, even tone.
2. Check that the diaphragm is giving a light support to the air stream.
3. Experiment with the air column to see which blowing angle gives the best result.
4. Check the amount of lower lip that is covering the embouchure hole; usually a coverage of about one third will produce a good result.

LET'S BEGUINE
(A duet for pupil and teacher)

Peter Wastall

In the style of a beguine

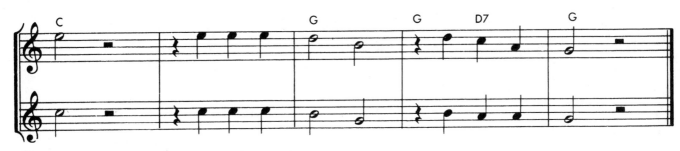

© Copyright 1979 by Boosey & Hawkes Music Publishers Ltd.

* Chord symbols for keyboard accompaniment

9

UNIT 3

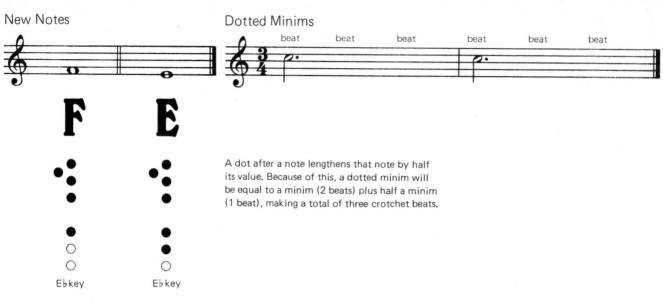

New Notes

F

E

Eb key

Eb key

Dotted Minims

A dot after a note lengthens that note by half its value. Because of this, a dotted minim will be equal to a minim (2 beats) plus half a minim (1 beat), making a total of three crotchet beats.

Exercise 1

Exercise 2

Exercise 3

Exercise 4

Musicianship

The ability to remember melodic phrases plays an important part in the development of musicianship. To help develop a melodic memory, try each week to memorise one of the shorter instrumental solos.

The grade 1 aural tests issued by the Associated Board of the Royal Schools of Music will help memory development and should be incorporated into the lesson at this stage.

SWIM, SWAN, SWIM!

Lively

Derek Hyde

© Copyright 1973 by Boosey & Hawkes Music Publishers Ltd.

CHORALE MELODY

At a moderate speed

German, 16th century

A MELODY IN PHRYGIAN MODE
No. 28 from "Mikrokosmos" Vol. 1

Fairly lively

Béla Bartók

© Copyright 1940 by Hawkes & Son (London) Ltd.

UNIT 4

Semibreve Rests

Ties

A semibreve rest is used to show any complete bar of rest, regardless of the number of beats in the bar. When it occurs you must examine the time-signature to find the number of beats to be counted. Compare the three examples.

A tie is a curved line placed over or under two notes of the same pitch. The tie joins the notes together making one continuous note. In order to produce one continuous note the second note must not be tongued.

Exercise 1

Exercise 2

Exercise 3

MARCH
"If all the world were paper"

Derek Hyde

In a bright march tempo

Tone development

1. Keep the top lip firm, and the lower lip slightly relaxed.
2. Don't allow the centre of the lips to pull inwards.
3. Check that the right hand little finger is on the E♭ key.
4. Sustain each pause note for as long as possible.

MEXICAN MADNESS

Peter Wastall

Lively

UNIT 5

New Notes

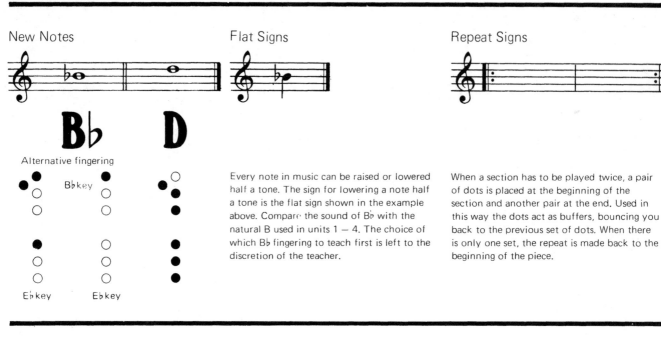

Flat Signs

Every note in music can be raised or lowered half a tone. The sign for lowering a note half a tone is the flat sign shown in the example above. Compare the sound of B♭ with the natural B used in units 1 — 4. The choice of which B♭ fingering to teach first is left to the discretion of the teacher.

Repeat Signs

When a section has to be played twice, a pair of dots is placed at the beginning of the section and another pair at the end. Used in this way the dots act as buffers, bouncing you back to the previous set of dots. When there is only one set, the repeat is made back to the beginning of the piece.

Exercise 1

Exercise 2

Exercise 3

Exercise 4

Musicianship

Articulation (the word used to describe tonguing in wind music) plays an important part in the creation of expression. It is the speech of music and can be thought of as the music equivalent of elocution. The tongue must be expressive, varying both the syllable formed and the strength of touch. In this unit concentrate on improving your articulation, using the pronunciation to give additional meaning to the phrases.

FFIGYSBREN

At a moderate speed

A traditional Welsh tune

CHORALE

Lively

A 16th century German melody

HAIL TO THE LORD'S ANOINTED

Slow and dignified

Johann Crüger

UNIT 6

Keys and Key-signatures

*Because of the key-signature both these notes must be played as B♭

Slurs

Italian Terms

When flat signs are placed at the beginning of each staff they are called a key-signature. Each flat is placed on a specific line or space indicating that every note with that letter name is to be played as if the flat were against the note. The two keys that use the key-signature with one flat are: F Major and D Minor. The Music in this unit is in F major.

A slur is a curved line placed over or under notes of different pitch. It indicates that the notes contained within the slur are to be played smoothly in one continuous breath. In order to do this only the first note is tongued.

Italian terms describe how fast a piece is to be played and how loud or soft the music should sound. The terms which describe how loud or soft the music should sound are usually abbreviated. A table of the abbreviations is printed in Unit 12 where this aspect of technique is developed.
A list of Italian terms is printed at the end of the book.

F Major

Exercise 1

Exercise 2

Exercise 3

CANTILENA

Andante

Adapted from a melody
by Johann Gabrielsky

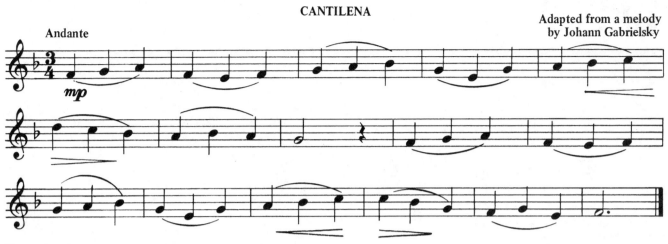

Tone development

By now it should be possible to play the note B with quite a 'rich' tone. The next exercise shows how to carry this rich tone down towards the low F. Points to think about are:

1. Diaphragm giving a light support to the air stream.
2. Facial muscles firm, but not gripping.

3. The soft inside part of the top lip driving the air stream towards the far edge of the embouchure hole.

DUO
Adapted from "St. Petersburg"

Dmitry Bortniansky

Andante

Teacher
Pupil

UNIT 7

Middle Octave Notes

E   F   G   A

Keys and Key-signatures

To produce the middle octave notes carry out the following drill:

1. Use the same fingering as for the lower octave.
2. Increase the breath support by firming the diaphragm.
3. Bring the jaw forward.
4. Reduce the size of the aperture by firming the muscles of the top lip.

The combined actions of 3 and 4 should result in the bottom lip covering a fraction more of the embouchure hole.

The two keys that have no flats (or sharps) in their key-signatures are: C Major and A Minor. The music in this unit illustrates C Major.

C Major

Exercise 1

Exercise 2

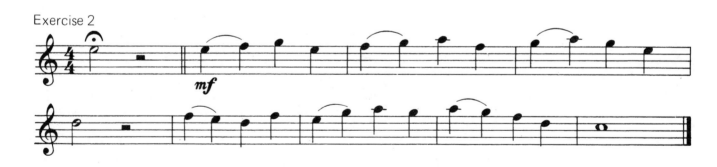

Exercise 3

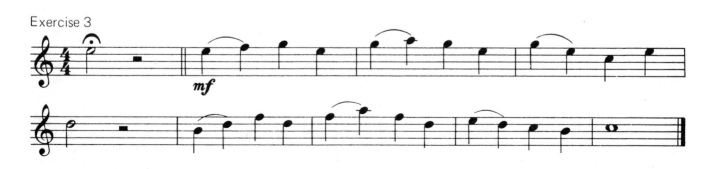

"AH VOUS DIRAI-JE, MAMAN"

Allegretto   A traditional French tune

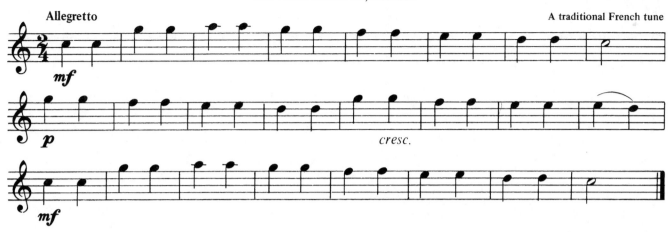

Tone development

1. Notes going up: bring the jaw smoothly forward, adjusting the blowing angle to produce a full middle octave sound.

2. Notes going down: draw the jaw gently backwards. adjusting the blowing angle to produce a full lower octave sound.

3. Repeat exercise (a) using the notes shown in exercises (b) and (c).

QUEM PASTORES

Moderato   A 14th century German melody

CHORALE

Andante   J. S. Bach

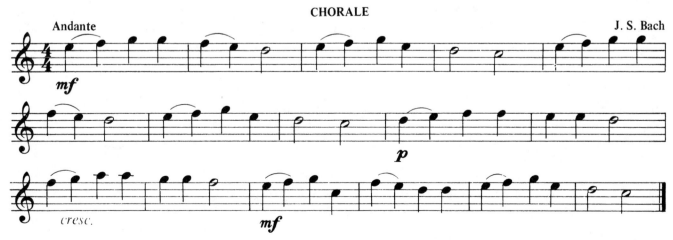

UNIT 8

Staccato Marks

When a dot is placed over or under a note it indicates that the note is to sound detached. To achieve this, the note is played shorter than its printed value, often producing a clipped effect, rather like saying the word TAP.

Quavers

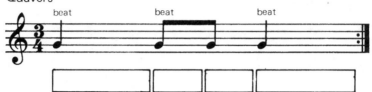

The value of a quaver is half a crotchet; it is printed with a tail on the end of its stem. For ease of reading, groups of quavers usually have their tails joined together.

Exercise 1

Exercise 2

Exercise 3

Scales and arpeggios

F Major, to be played from memory

Aids to music reading

When you play quavers read them like a two-syllable word. For example, when you read the word 'Doctor', you don't read 'Doc' then 'tor', you read 'Doctor'. This "block" reading skill should be developed at the earliest possible stage of music reading. To help this development, each time quavers occur, make a conscious effort to read both notes at the same time.

RIGAUDON

Allegretto   Henry Purcell

CORUMBA

Lively (in the style of a bossa-nova)   Peter Wastall

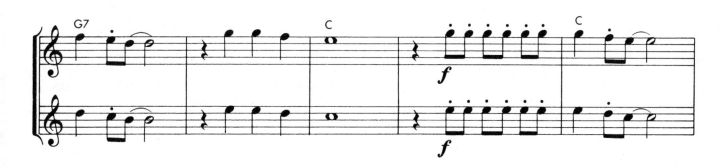

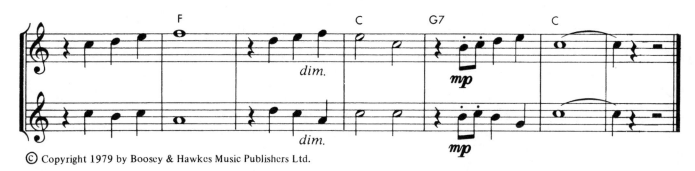

CONCERT PIECES FOR UNITS 1-8

Piano accompaniments to the concert pieces are available in a separate accompaniment book. These should be used to provide experience in playing with an accompanist. 'Minuetto' by Hook 'Soliloquy' by Hyde and 'Chorus' by Gluck are examples of music that have been set for early grade examinations.

MINUETTO
from Sonata No. 3, op. 99

JAMES HOOK
(1746–1827)

CHORUS
from "Paris and Helen"

C. W. GLUCK
(1714–1787)
arr. PETER WASTALL

SOLILOQUY

DEREK HYDE

HUMMING SONG
from "Album for the young" op. 68

ROBERT SCHUMANN
(1810–1856)
arr. PETER WASTALL

UNIT 9

New Notes

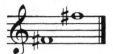

F#

Eb key

Sharp Signs

The sign for raising a note by half a tone is called a sharp sign. Like the flat sign it can be placed immediately before the note it affects, or it can be placed at the beginning of each staff to form a key-signature.

A New Key-signature

*Because of the key-signature both these notes must be played as F♯.

The two keys that use the key-signature with one sharp are: G Major and E Minor. The music in this unit illustrates G Major.

G Major

Exercise 1

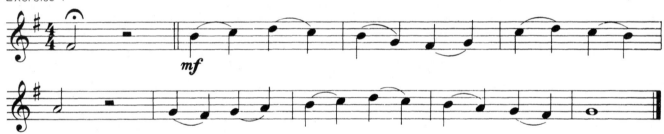

Exercise 2

Exercise 3

Scales and arpeggios

G Major, to be played from memory.

Finger technique

1. After playing D, the right hand little finger must return to the E♭ key. This is particularly important when D is followed by E. During this unit, concentrate on improving this part of your finger technique.

2. When moving from D to C, the flute must remain correctly balanced. The main control points are: right hand thumb and little finger giving a forward thrust; left hand index finger acting as a midway support; the chin counteracting the push of the right hand. Check these points when playing the pieces.

MINUET

Adapted from a minuet by J. S. Bach

LAND OF OUR FATHERS

A traditional Welsh tune

UNIT 10

Accent signs

Dotted crotchets

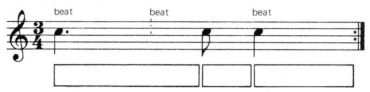

An accent sign placed over or under a note means that the note must be given a strong attack with the tongue. Often this strong attack is combined with a little 'punch' from the diaphragm.

Since a dot after a note lengthens that note by half its value, the value of a dotted crotchet will be one and a half crotchet beats, the same length of sound as three quavers added together. Look at the example, then study the similarity of bars 2 and 3 in the first exercise.

Exercise 1

Exercise 2

Exercise 3

THE EMPEROR OF GERMANY'S MARCH

Jeremiah Clarke

Tone development

1. Sustain the pause note for as long as possible, trying at all times to achieve a rich, full tone.
2. Keep the lips still during the first rest.
3. Start the second note with the tone developed in bar 1.
4. Tune the interval (a perfect fifth) by using the jaw: a forward movement to raise the pitch, a backward movement to lower the pitch.
5. Repeat exercise (a) using the notes shown in exercises (b) (c) and (d).

FANFARE

Nicholas Chédeville

UNIT 11

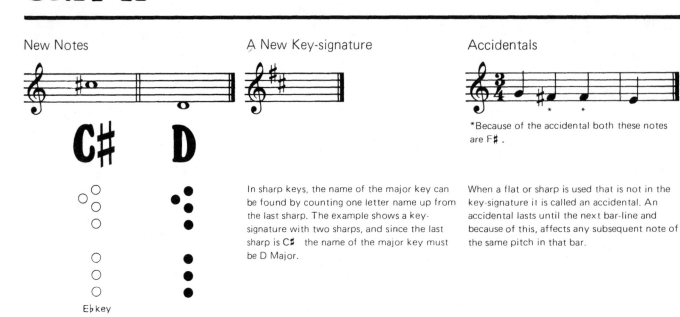

New Notes

C#   D

Eb key

A New Key-signature

In sharp keys, the name of the major key can be found by counting one letter name up from the last sharp. The example shows a key-signature with two sharps, and since the last sharp is C♯ the name of the major key must be D Major.

Accidentals

*Because of the accidental both these notes are F♯.

When a flat or sharp is used that is not in the key-signature it is called an accidental. An accidental lasts until the next bar-line and because of this, affects any subsequent note of the same pitch in that bar.

Exercise 1

mf

Exercise 2

mp

Exercise 3

p   *cresc.*   *f*

Scales and arpeggios

D Major, to be played from memory.

Tone development

1. Listen carefully and tune the octave.
2. Use the second bar to develop a strong middle octave sound.
3. Keep the lips still during bar 3.

4. Start bar 4 with a tone identical to that developed in bar 2.
5. Repeat exercise (a) using the notes shown in exercises (b) (c) and (d).

A LITTLE PIECE

Antonio Diabelli

LULLABY

Franz Schubert

UNIT 12

Natural Signs

Italian Terms

pp   very soft   **ff**   very loud

p   soft   **f**   loud

mp   moderately soft   **mf**   moderately loud

————————— gradually softer   ————————— gradually louder

A natural sign is used to cancel a flat or sharp. Since it is a type of accidental, it will only last for the bar in which it is printed. However, if a note that has been altered occurs again in the next bar, an additional accidental is often used to confirm that the note has returned to its original pitch.

Italian terms also describe the mood of a piece, changes of speed and large repeats such as da capo. As with Italian terms introduced earlier, English translations can be found at the end of the book.

A table of Italian terms which show how loud or soft the music should sound is printed above. It should be used in conjunction with the tuning technique introduced in this unit.

Exercise 1

Exercise 2

Exercise 3

MINUET

Allegretto

G. P. Telemann

Musicianship

Crescendos and diminuendos play an important part in creating expression but need careful use since they also have an effect on tuning. Basically, a crescendo (produced by increasing the air pressure) will make a note go sharp; and a diminuendo (produced by reducing the air pressure) will make a note go flat.

To stabilise the tuning, the jaw is drawn back in crescendo, and brought forward in diminuendo.

DUETTO No. 1
(2nd movt.)

Andante

Johann Gabrielsky

D. C. al Fine

UNIT 13

New Notes

Quaver Rests

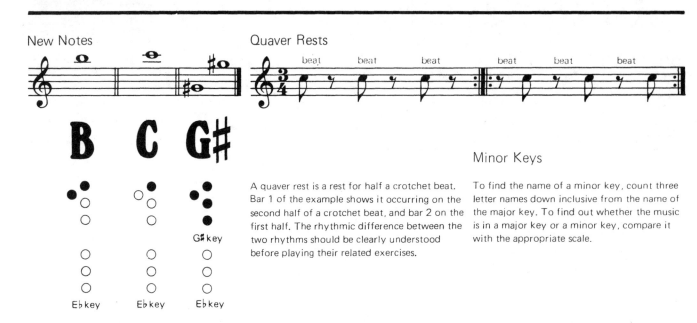

B C G#

G# key

E♭ key   E♭ key   E♭ key

A quaver rest is a rest for half a crotchet beat. Bar 1 of the example shows it occurring on the second half of a crotchet beat, and bar 2 on the first half. The rhythmic difference between the two rhythms should be clearly understood before playing their related exercises.

Minor Keys

To find the name of a minor key, count three letter names down inclusive from the name of the major key. To find out whether the music is in a major key or a minor key, compare it with the appropriate scale.

A Minor

Exercise 1

mp   *cresc.*

f

Exercise 2

mp   *cresc.*

f

mp   *cresc.*   *f*

Scales and arpeggios

A Minor (harmonic form) to be played from memory.

Scales and arpeggios

C Major, to be played from memory.

Tone development

1. Use the pause note to develop a strong lower octave sound.
2. Start bar 3 with a minimum air pressure; then crescendo, stabilising the tuning with the jaw.
3. At the peak of the crescendo strive to achieve the same sound as that developed during the pause.
4. Repeat exercise (a) using the notes shown in exercises (b) and (c).

ETUDE

Moderato

Antonio Diabelli

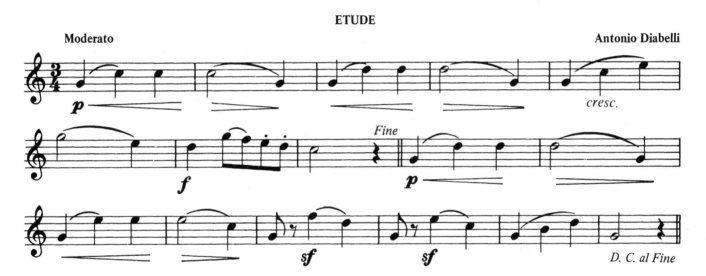

AYLESFORD'S PIECE

Animato

G. F. Handel

33

UNIT 14

Compound Time

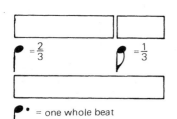

$\bigcirc = \frac{2}{3}$ $\bigcirc = \frac{1}{3}$

 = one whole beat

When the natural pulse of a piece divides itself into thirds of a beat the music is said to be in compound time. The various notes retain the same value in relation to each other; for instance there are still two quavers in a crotchet, but their value in relation to the beat is changed to the values shown in the example.

Compound Time-signatures

To show the new note values a new set of time-signatures is used. The example shows six-eight, indicating two dotted crotchet beats in a bar. A chart showing the complete range of compound time-signatures and how they are applied is printed at the end of the book.

Exercise 1

Exercise 2

Exercise 3

MARMOTTE

Allegretto

L. van Beethoven

Aids to music reading

When reading notes which are thirds of a beat, read them as if they were three-syllable words. As an example of this, try the first exercise thinking the word TENTATIVE as you play each group. When playing the pieces, apply this reading principle to all rhythmic groups contained within one beat.

DUETTO IN A MINOR

Andante grazioso

Adapted from a duet
by Benoit Berbiguier

UNIT 15

New Notes

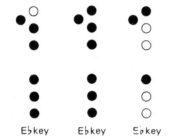

Eb · Eb · A#

Eb key · Eb key · Eb key

Double Names for Notes

A# = Bb   C# = Db   D# = Eb   F# = Gb   G# = Ab

The interval between A and B is one whole tone. Since a sharp raises a note by half a tone and a flat lowers a note by half a tone, it follows that A# and Bb are different names for the same note. Double names can be given to all the flats and sharps learned so far.

A New Key-signature

In flat keys, the name of the major key can be found by counting four letter names down from the last flat. The key-signature of exercise 1 has Bb and Eb, therefore the name of the major key must be Bb Major.

Exercise 1

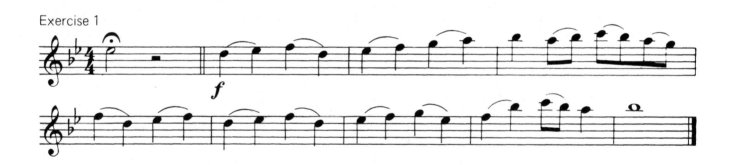

Exercise 2

Exercise 3

Scales and arpeggios

Bb Major, to be played from memory.

F Major , to be played from memory

Finger technique

1. Middle octave Bb is fingered the same as lower octave Bb, and in most pieces either of the fingerings shown in unit 5 are possible. However, exercise (a) illustrates a typical finger pattern where the Bb key will produce a smoother result.

2. When Bb or A# occur in a chromatic passage — see exercises (b) and (c) — the fingering shown in this unit is the one that must be used. The chromatic run should be memorised, so that when needed it can be played fluently.

ARIA

Allegretto

Friedrich Gluck

mf *cantabile*

WALTZ

Andante

Franz Schubert

mp

mf

UNIT 16

Tenuto signs

1st and 2nd time bars

A tenuto sign placed over or under a note means that the note is to be played with a lingering pressure. Usually it is also associated with a type of tonguing where one syllable is added to another without any noticable break in the air stream.

Sometimes the ending of a repeated section is altered the second time through. When this occurs 1st and 2nd time bars are used. The example is taken from "Ein' feste Burg", in which bars 1 - 4 are played quite normally the first time through, but when they are repeated the first time bar is omitted and the second time bar played instead.

Exercise 1

Exercise 2

Exercise 3

EIN' FESTE BURG

Andante moderato

A chorale by M. Luther
adapted by J. S. Bach

Musicianship

Sometimes the general character of a piece suggests that many of the notes should be played staccato. When this occurs, the dots on top of the notes are often omitted, leaving it to the instrumentalist to interpret the music in a staccato style. The "Duo" by Chédeville is an example of this.

DUO IN D MINOR

Allegro

Esprit Chédeville

39

CONCERT PIECES FOR UNITS 9-16

As with earlier concert pieces, piano accompaniments should be used to provide experience in playing with an accompanist. 'Lullaby' by Szelenyi and 'Minuet' by Mozart are examples of music that has been set for early grade examinations.

MINUET
from Divertimento No. 2, K.229

W. A. MOZART
(1756 – 1791)
arr. PETER WASTALL

LULLABY
from "24 Easy Concert Pieces"

ISTVÁN SZELÉNYI
(1904 – 1972)

MELODY

from the song "Ich Liebe Dich"

L. van BEETHOVEN
(1770 − 1827)

UNIT 17

New Notes

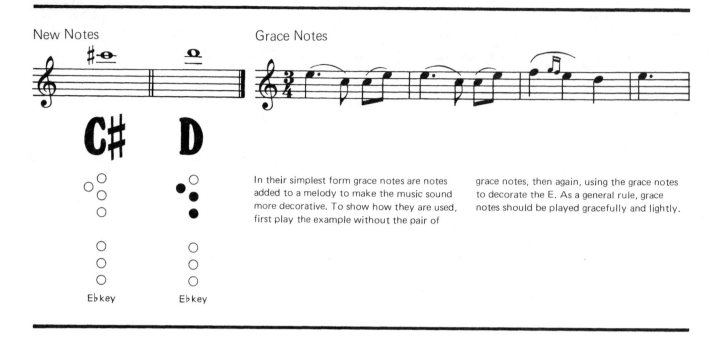

Grace Notes

C#   D

Eb key   Eb key

In their simplest form grace notes are notes added to a melody to make the music sound more decorative. To show how they are used, first play the example without the pair of grace notes, then again, using the grace notes to decorate the E. As a general rule, grace notes should be played gracefully and lightly.

STUDY No.1

Adapted from a study by Giuseppe Gariboldi

PASTORALE
No. 24 from "Mikrokosmos" Vol. 1

Moderato

Béla Bartók

Tone development

1. Maintain an even dynamic level throughout each exercise.

2. Use a supple reduction of the lip aperture to change the octave.

3. Repeat each exercise using the notes C, C# and D.

WALTZ

Andantino

Johannes Brahms

UNIT 18

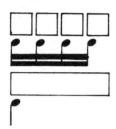

Semiquavers

Syncopation

The value of a semiquaver is a quarter of a crotchet; it is printed with two tails on the end of its stem. As with quavers, all the tails contained in one beat can be joined together.

A new rhythm, called syncopation, is produced when strongly accented notes occur between the beats instead of coinciding with them.

As shown in the duet, the surrounding quavers are usually played staccato to help bounce the syncopated notes off the beat.

Exercise 1

Exercise 2

Scales and arpeggios

 G major, to be played from memory

44

AN OLD HUNGARIAN DANCE
from "Clarinet Music for Beginners"

Pál Károlyi
(born 1934)

Moderato

Aids to music reading

With blocks of four semiquavers, read each group as you would a four-syllable word. Start with passages that are easy to finger (such as the two exercises shown opposite) and make a conscious effort to read each block of four semiquavers as a single unit.

A SYNCOPATED DUET

François Garnier

Allegretto

UNIT 19

A New Note

E

Eb key

Dotted Quavers

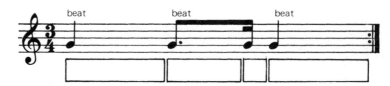

A dotted quaver, or its equivalent rest, lasts for three quarters of a crotchet beat. Usually it is combined with a single semiquaver since this completes the beat.

STUDY No.2

Adapted from a study
by Giuseppe Gariboldi

LARGO

Aids to music reading

The reading technique for a single semiquaver is to group the semiquaver with the note which follows. In lively movements a useful way to achieve this is to pronounce the two notes as if saying the word TODAY. As an example, play the first note of the "Soldier's March" by Schumann, then think TODAY as you play the next two notes. This reading technique can be used every time a dotted rhythm occurs.

SOLDIER'S MARCH

UNIT 20

Semiquaver Rests

Note-patterns using Semiquavers

The semiquaver rest is a rest for a quarter of a crotchet beat. Notice that it is similar to the semiquaver note, being printed with two tails. Examples of the semiquaver rest can be found in the duet.

By combining semiquavers with quavers several new rhythm patterns can be formed. The examples should be studied carefully before playing the exercises.

Exercise 1

Exercise 2

Scales and arpeggios

A Minor (harmonic form) to be played from memory

ÉCOSSAISE

L. van Beethoven

Musicianship

As you play the "Duetto" by Devienne, notice that the general character is one of smoothness. To achieve this smoothness, use a very gentle type of tonguing; rather like pronouncing the dyllable DAH. When playing in this manner, we say we are interpreting the music in a legato style. Compare the style with that needed for playing the Beethoven "Écossaise", where the mood suggests that the quavers be played with a ringing, bouncy type of staccato.

DUETTO IN D MINOR

François Devienne

UNIT 21

New Notes

Three-eight Time

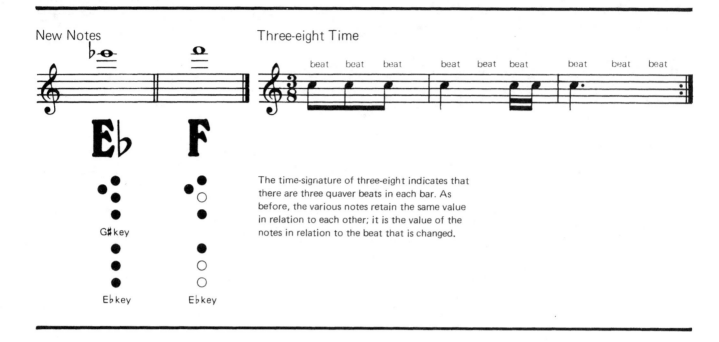

E♭ **F**

G♯ key

E♭ key   E♭ key

The time-signature of three-eight indicates that
there are three quaver beats in each bar. As
before, the various notes retain the same value
in relation to each other; it is the value of the
notes in relation to the beat that is changed.

STUDY NO. 3

Adapted from a study
by Giuseppe Gariboldi

Allegretto grazioso

GERMAN DANCE

L. van Beethoven

Tone development

1. Start with the best possible tone.
2. Having achieved a good tone, spread it to the note below.

3. Use the tiny muscles at the lip centre to help drive the air stream towards the far edge of the embouchure hole.

4. Continue exercises (b) (c) and (d) down to the low E♭.

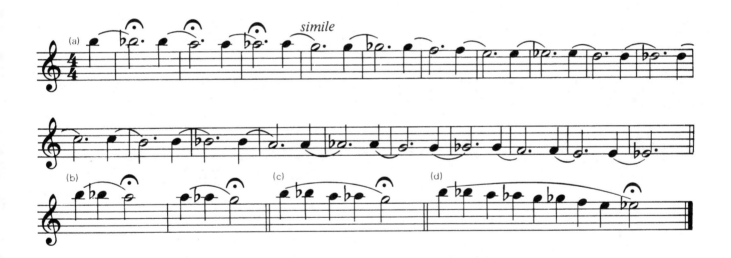

MINUETTO

Antonio Vivaldi

UNIT 22

Triplets

Two-two Time

A triplet can be defined as 'three notes played in the time of two notes of the same value' (for instance, three quavers played in the time of two quavers). The number 3 is placed over or under the notes to show the momentary change of note value.

The time-signature of two-two indicates that there are two minim beats in each bar. The value of the notes in relation to the beat is shown in the example. Sometimes, two-two is called Alla Breve.

Exercise 1

Scales and arpeggios

F Major, to be played from memory.

D Minor (harmonic form), to be played from memory

B Minor (harmonic form), to be played from memory.

ARIA

G. F. Handel

Musicianship

Both pieces in this unit have performing directions relating to their mood: the Handel "Aria" is marked dolce espressivo, and the Loeillet duet grazioso. As you practise, try to create these moods using the appropriate staccato and legato styles of playing. In the "Aria", the repeated notes create good opportunities for expressive tenuto playing; the important thing to remember is that performing directions are a starting point for creating your own expression.

GAVOTTE

J. B. Loeillet

UNIT 23

New Notes

Changes of Time-signature

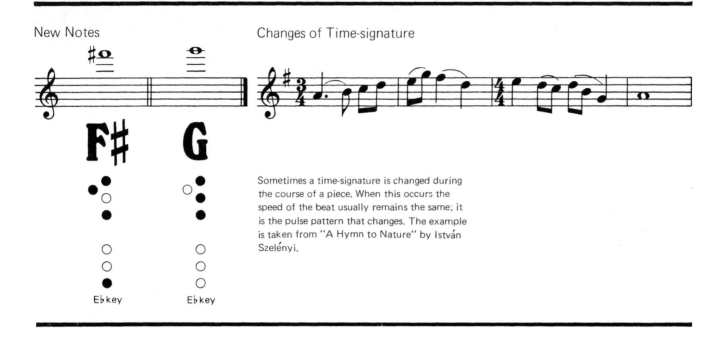

F#   G

Eb key   Eb key

Sometimes a time-signature is changed during the course of a piece. When this occurs the speed of the beat usually remains the same; it is the pulse pattern that changes. The example is taken from "A Hymn to Nature" by István Szelényi.

STUDY NO. 4

Adapted from a study by Giuseppe Gariboldi

A HYMN TO NATURE
from "24 Easy Pieces for Violin and Piano"

István Szelényi
(1904-1972)

Tone development

1. Start with a good tone, then spread it to the note above.
2. Gradually reduce the size of the aperture by firming the lip muscles.
3. Experiment with the angle of the air stream to find the best upper octave sound.
4. Maintain a strong breath support throughout.
5. Repeat the exercise (as in unit 21) using groups of 3, 5 and 9.

ALMANDE

Giles Farnaby

UNIT 24

Acciaccaturas

Rests of Several Bars

1	2	3	(1st bar)
2	2	3	(2nd bar)
3	2	3	(3rd bar)

An acciaccatura is a small grace note with a stroke through its stem. It should be played on the beat and as short as possible.

When a rest of several bars is required only one bar is used; a black line is usually drawn in this bar, and the number of complete bars to be counted placed on top. The example is taken from the concert piece on p. 58.

Adapted from a study by Wilhelm Popp

Exercise 1

Scales and arpeggios

G Major, to be played from memory.

E Minor (harmonic form), to be played from memory.

D Major, to be played from memory.

Antonio Diabelli

Finger technique

1. Care should be taken when playing upper octave F♯ in flat keys (see the scale of G minor); for correct tuning, the thumb must be on the B♮ plate.

2. When middle octave D occurs as an acciaccatura to C, the trill fingering for D (C plus the first trill key) is normally used. An example occurs in the "Andante" by Diabelli.

FANFARE

Marc-Antoine Charpentier

CONCERT PIECES FOR UNITS 17-24

'Air' by Purcell and 'Serenade' by Haydn are examples of music that have been set for early grade examinations.

AIR

from "H. Purcell: Two Pieces"
arr. Roland Revell

HENRY PURCELL
(1659-1695)

SERENADE

from *"Classical Album for Flute"*
arr. Harold Perry

JOSEPH HAYDN
(1732-1809)

Andante cantabile

PIECE No. 5
from "Eight Pieces for Organ"

CÉSAR FRANCK
(1822-1890)
arr. PETER WASTALL

ADAGIO
from "Sonatina for Flute and Piano"

PÁL JÁRDÁNYI
(1920-1966)

BASIC FINGERING CHART

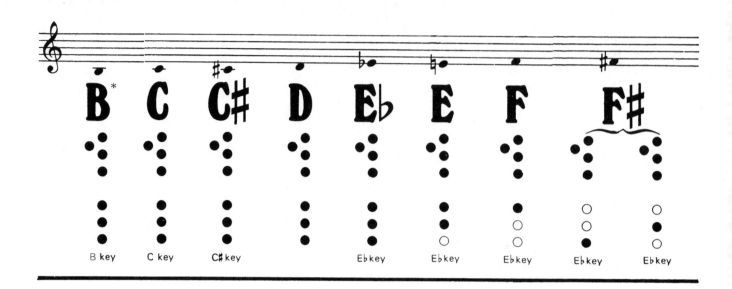

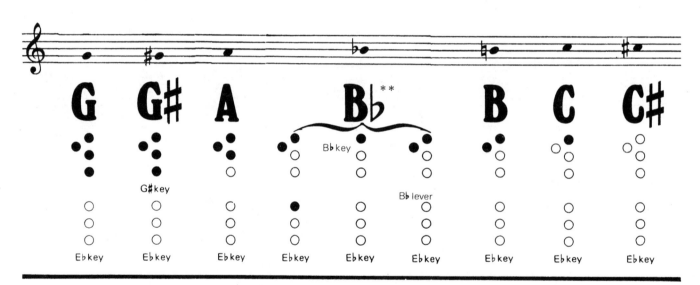

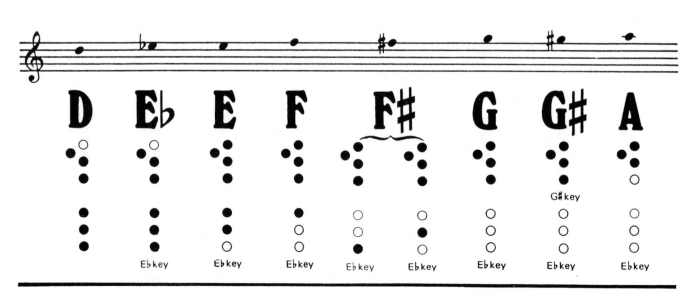

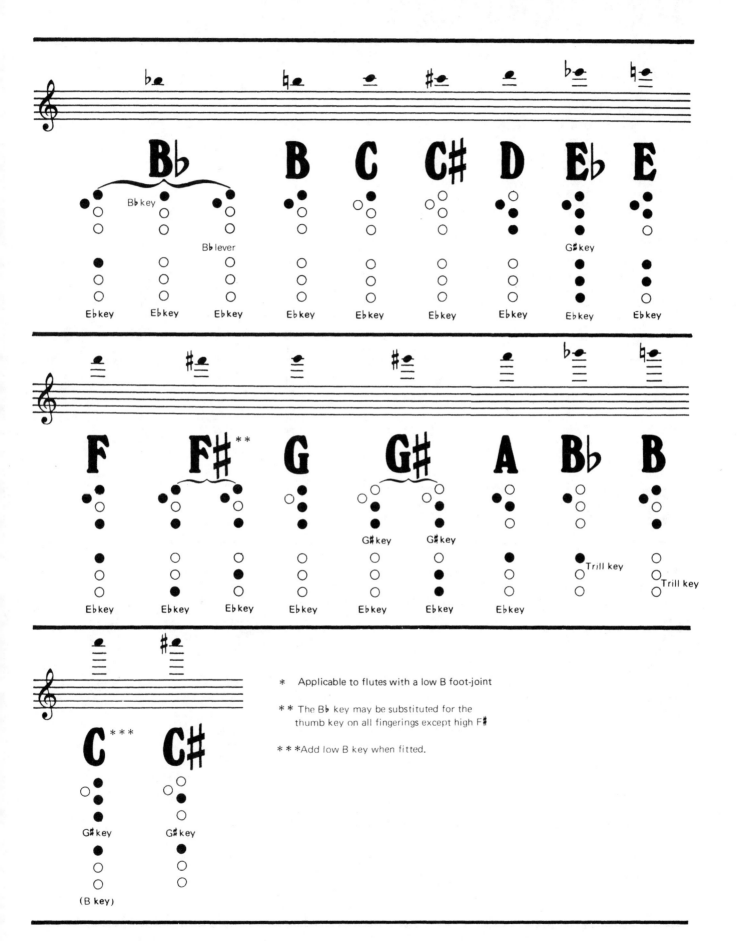

* Applicable to flutes with a low B foot-joint

** The B♭ key may be substituted for the thumb key on all fingerings except high F#

*** Add low B key when fitted.

TIME SIGNATURES

1. Look up the time signature

2. Look in the left hand column to find the number of beats in each bar.

3. Look in the top row above the time signature to find the type of note that equals one beat.

	Simple time			Compound time		
Value of each beat (type of note)	𝅗𝅥	♩	♪	𝅗𝅥.	♩.	♪.
Value of each beat as a fraction of a semibreve	$\frac{1}{2}$	$\frac{1}{4}$	$\frac{1}{8}$	$\frac{3}{4}$	$\frac{3}{8}$	$\frac{3}{16}$
2 beats in each bar	$\frac{2}{2}$	$\frac{2}{4}$	$\frac{2}{8}$	$\frac{6}{4}$	$\frac{6}{8}$	$\frac{6}{16}$
3 beats in each bar	$\frac{3}{2}$	$\frac{3}{4}$	$\frac{3}{8}$	$\frac{9}{4}$	$\frac{9}{8}$	$\frac{9}{16}$
4 beats in each bar	$\frac{4}{2}$	$\frac{4}{4}$	$\frac{4}{8}$	$\frac{12}{4}$	$\frac{12}{8}$	$\frac{12}{16}$

ITALIAN TERMS

A tempo Resume the normal speed.
Accelerando Becoming gradually faster.
Adagio Slow, leisurely.
Agitato Agitated.
Alla marcia In the style of a march.
Allargando Broadening out.
Allegretto Slightly slower than Allegro.
Allegro Lively, reasonably fast.
Andante (lit. walking) At a moderate pace.
Andantino A little andante.
Animato Animated.
Cantabile In a singing style.
Con With.
Crescendo *(cresc.)* Becoming louder.
Da Capo (D.C.) al Fine Back to the beginning and finish at the word Fine.
Dal Segno (D. S.) From the sign 𝄋
Deciso Decisively, firmly.
Diminuendo *(dim.)* Becoming gradually softer.

Dolce Sweetly.
E, Ed And.
Espressivo *(espress.)* With expression, with feeling.
Forte (*f*) Loud.
Fortissimo (*ff*) Very loud.
Grazioso Gracefully.
Largo Slow and stately, broad.
Larghetto Less slow than Largo.
Legato Smoothly.
Leggiero Lightly.
Lento Slowly.
Maestoso Majestically.
Meno mosso Less movement.
Mezzo forte (*mf*) Moderately loud.
Mezzo piano (*mp*) Moderately soft.
Moderato Moderate time.
Molto Much.
Moto Movement.
Non troppo Not too much.

Pianissimo (*pp*) Very soft.
Piano (*p*) Soft.
Più mosso More movement, quicker.
Poco a poco Little by little (gradually).
Presto Very quick.
Quasi As if, almost.
Rallentando (rall.) Becoming gradually slower.
Ritenuto (rit.) Hold back (slower at once).
Rubato Flexibly.
Semplice Simple.
Sempre Always.
Sforzando (*sf*, *sfz*) Forcing, accented.
Solenne Solemn.
Sonore Sonorous, full toned.
Sostenuto Sustained.
Spirito Spirit, life, energy.
Tempo I Resume the original speed.
Tranquillo Quietly.
Un poco A little.
Vivace Lively, quick.

Printed by
Halstan & Co. Ltd., Amersham, Bucks., England